SLEEP DISORDERS

MENTAL ILLNESSES AND DISORDERS

Alzheimer's Disease
Anxiety Disorders
Attention-Deficit Hyperactivity Disorder
Autism Spectrum Disorders
Bipolar Disorder
Depression
Disruptive Behavior Disorders
Drug and Alcohol Dependence
Eating Disorders
Obsessive-Compulsive Disorder
Post-Traumatic Stress Disorder
Schizophrenia
Sleep Disorders

MENTAL ILLNESSES AND DISORDERS
Awareness and Understanding

SLEEP
DISORDERS

H.W. Poole

SERIES CONSULTANT

ANNE S. WALTERS, PhD

Chief Psychologist, Emma Pendleton Bradley Hospital

Clinical Associate Professor, Alpert Medical School/Brown University

MASON CREST

Mason Crest
450 Parkway Drive, Suite D
Broomall, PA 19008
www.masoncrest.com

MTM Publishing, Inc.
435 West 23rd Street, #8C
New York, NY 10011
www.mtmpublishing.com

President: Valerie Tomaselli
Vice President, Book Development: Hilary Poole
Designer: Annemarie Redmond
Copyeditor: Peter Jaskowiak
Editorial Assistant: Andrea St. Aubin

Series ISBN: 978-1-4222-3364-1
ISBN: 978-1-4222-3376-4
Ebook ISBN: 978-1-4222-8577-0

Library of Congress Cataloging-in-Publication Data

Poole, Hilary W., author.
  Sleep disorders / by H.W. Poole.
      pages cm. — (Mental illnesses and disorders: awareness and understanding)
  Includes bibliographical references and index.
  ISBN 978-1-4222-3376-4 (hardback) — ISBN 978-1-4222-3364-1 (series) —
ISBN 978-1-4222-8577-0 (ebook)
  1. Sleep disorders—Juvenile literature. 2. Sleep—Juvenile literature. I. Title.
  RC547.P66 2016
  616.8'498—dc23
                                        2015006830

Printed and bound in the United States of America.

First printing
9 8 7 6 5 4 3 2 1

TABLE OF CONTENTS

Key Icons to Look for:

Words to Understand: These words with their easy-to-understand definitions will increase the reader's understanding of the text, while building vocabulary skills.

Sidebars: This boxed material within the main text allows readers to build knowledge, gain insights, explore possibilities, and broaden their perspectives by weaving together additional information to provide realistic and holistic perspectives.

Research Projects: Readers are pointed toward areas of further inquiry connected to each chapter. Suggestions are provided for projects that encourage deeper research and analysis.

Text-Dependent Questions: These questions send the reader back to the text for more careful attention to the evidence presented there.

Series Glossary of Key Terms: This back-of-the-book glossary contains terminology used throughout the series. Words found here increase the reader's ability to read and comprehend higher-level books and articles in this field.

People who cope with mental illnesses and disorders deserve our empathy and respect.

(istockphoto/digitalskillet)

Introduction to the Series

According to the National Institute of Mental Health, in 2012 there were an estimated 45 million people in the United States suffering from mental illness, or 19 percent of all US adults. A separate 2011 study found that among children, almost one in five suffer from some form of mental illness or disorder. The nature and level of impairment varies widely. For example, children and adults with anxiety disorders may struggle with a range of symptoms, from a constant state of worry about both real and imagined events to a complete inability to leave the house. Children or adults with schizophrenia might experience periods when the illness is well controlled by medication and therapies, but there may also be times when they must spend time in a hospital for their own safety and the safety of others. For every person with mental illness who makes the news, there are many more who do not, and these are the people that we must learn more about and help to feel accepted, and even welcomed, in this world of diversity.

It is not easy to have a mental illness in this country. Access to mental health services remains a significant issue. Many states and some private insurers have "opted out" of providing sufficient coverage for mental health treatment. This translates to limits on the amount of sessions or frequency of treatment, inadequate rates for providers, and other problems that make it difficult for people to get the care they need.

Meanwhile, stigma about mental illness remains widespread. There are still whispers about "bad parenting," or "the other side of the tracks." The whisperers imply that mental illness is something you bring upon yourself, or something that someone does to you. Obviously, mental illness can be exacerbated by an adverse event such as trauma or parental instability. But there is just as much truth to the biological bases of mental illness. No one is made schizophrenic by ineffective parenting, for example, or by engaging in "wild" behavior as an adolescent. Mental illness is a complex interplay of genes, biology, and the environment, much like many physical illnesses.

People with mental illness are brave soldiers, really. They fight their illness every day, in all of the settings of their lives. When people with an anxiety disorder graduate from college, you know that they worked very hard to get there—harder, perhaps, than those who did not struggle with a psychiatric issue. They got up every day with a pit in their stomach about facing the world, and they worried about their finals more than their classmates. When they had to give a presentation in class, they thought their world was going to end and that they would faint, or worse, in front of everyone. But they fought back, and they kept going. Every day. That's bravery, and that is to be respected and congratulated.

These books were written to help young people get the facts about mental illness. Facts go a long way to dispel stigma. Knowing the facts gives students the opportunity to help others to know and understand. If your student lives with someone with mental illness, these books can help students know a bit more about what to expect. If they are concerned about someone, or even about themselves, these books are meant to provide some answers and a place to start.

The topics covered in this series are those that seem most relevant for middle schoolers—disorders that they are most likely to come into contact with or to be curious about. Schizophrenia is a rare illness, but it is an illness with many misconceptions and inaccurate portrayals in media. Anxiety and depressive disorders, on the other hand, are quite common. Most of our youth have likely had personal experience of anxiety or depression, or knowledge of someone who struggles with these symptoms.

As a teacher or a librarian, thank you for taking part in dispelling myths and bringing facts to your children and students. Thank you for caring about the brave soldiers who live and work with mental illness. These reference books are for all of them, and also for those of us who have the good fortune to work with and know them.

—Anne S. Walters, PhD
Chief Psychologist, Emma Pendleton Bradley Hospital
Clinical Professor, Alpert Medical School/Brown University

CHAPTER ONE

SLEEP—WHAT IS IT GOOD FOR?

 Words to Understand

circadian: natural process that happens on a 24-hour cycle.

deprivation: a hurtful lack of something important.

insomnia: inability to fall asleep and/or stay asleep.

paralysis: inability to move.

rhythm: a repeating order of some activity or process.

3:12 am...

It's very late, but you can't fall asleep. You lie in bed and stare at the ceiling. You start thinking about how tired you'll be tomorrow. You know sleep is important because adults say so all the time. You worry that you'll feel lousy all day.

You know that worrying just makes things worse. So you close your eyes and try to relax. You count imaginary sheep in your head. You lie there for what feels like hours. You look at the clock again.

3:25 am...

When you have trouble sleeping, thinking about how you can't sleep makes you feel even worse.

This inability to fall asleep is called **insomnia**, and it happens to everyone once in a while. As long as it doesn't go on for

A LIFETIME OF SLEEP

Most people spend about a third of their lives sleeping. If a person sleeps eight hours every night, then by the time she is 15 years old, she will have spent a full 5 years asleep. By the time she's 75 years old, she'll have slept for 25 years.

That sounds like a lot, but some animals sleep even more. Some armadillos, opossums, and sloths spend as much of 80 percent of their lives sleeping!

many nights, it's nothing to worry about. But if you have insomnia often, you could have a health problem.

Everyone needs sleep, but what is it, anyway? Why do we need it, and why can sleep sometimes be so hard to get?

What Is Sleep?

Sleep is a time of physical rest. Our bodies are mostly still, and our eyes are usually closed. Our minds are not aware of the outside world. But sleep is a temporary state. Someone who is asleep can wake up.

People once thought that the brain stopped working when people were asleep. It was thought that the brain was resting along with the body. Today we know the opposite is true. The brain of a sleeping person is actually very busy!

Scientists tell us there are two types of sleep, each with a different level of brain activity: rapid eye movement (REM)

DANGEROUSLY TIRED

According to a poll by the National Sleep Foundation, 60 percent of adult drivers in America have driven a vehicle while feeling sleepy. Almost 37 percent admitted to falling asleep while driving. That means about 117 million people have driven while sleepy, and more than 72 million have actually fallen asleep.

Studies have shown that sleep-related automobile accidents kill more young people than accidents linked to alcohol.

Sleep **deprivation** has also contributed to some major disasters. Both the worst nuclear accident in US history (Three Mile Island, Pennsylvania, 1979) and the giant 1989 Exxon Valdez oil spill in Alaska were partly caused by someone who had not had enough sleep.

sleep, which is when people dream, and non-rapid eye movement (NREM) sleep, which does not involve dreaming.

In order to feel rested, our bodies need to go back and forth between REM and NREM sleep. This is called the sleep cycle. Most people experience four or five sleep cycles in a normal night's sleep, although this can vary.

The Sleep Cycle: NREM

NREM sleep has four stages. Stage 1 is that drowsy state when you move from being awake to falling asleep. Your eyelids feel heavy; your muscles begin to relax; your heart rate and breathing slow; you feel yourself drifting away. Stage 1 sleep normally lasts up to ten minutes and is a state from which you can be easily wakened.

Stage 2 sleep is a very light sleep. Your eyes are closed; your heart and breathing rates slow even more; your muscles relax. But you can still be wakened easily.

Stages 3 and 4 are the deepest type of sleep and the most difficult to wake from. These stages provide the kind of rest that best restores our bodies and minds. Most people reach stage 3 about 20 minutes after lying down. They usually reach stage 4, the deepest type of sleep, within about an hour.

The Sleep Cycle: REM

If you watch someone sleeping, you can tell if they have entered REM sleep by watching their eyes. Their eyes dart from

Experts believe that REM sleep is an important part of brain development.

HOW MUCH SLEEP DO YOU NEED?

You've probably heard that eight hours is the "right" amount of sleep. You may also have heard that the best time for that sleep is between 10:00 p.m. and 6:00 a.m. That is basically true. Most doctors would consider eight hours of sleep during the night to be ideal. There are lots of variations, however.

People have different sleep needs at different stages in life. For example, most newborn babies only sleep for a few hours at a time, but they do it all day long. Teenagers often need longer periods of sleep than most adults. On the other hand, elderly people tend to sleep less.

Within these trends, each individual is different. In fact, researchers have found that there really are "early birds" and "night owls," people who are at their best at particular parts of the day.

So how much sleep do *you* need? Your body is probably trying to tell you. Think about how you feel when you wake up. If you can wake up feeling refreshed, not tired or groggy, that's a good sign. If you get through your day without feeling tired, you've probably gotten a good amount of sleep.

back and forth beneath their closed eyelids. This occurs only during the part of the sleep cycle called REM sleep.

REM sleep begins after you've passed through the deeper sleep stages (Stages 3 and 4) and moved back into a lighter sleep stage again. Once in a lighter sleep stage, our brains go to work. Scientists believe that REM sleep helps us sort through our memories and emotions. People usually enter REM sleep about 90 minutes or so after they first fall asleep.

REM sleep is an active sleep phase for our brains, but our bodies remain still. Have you ever woken up during a nightmare and felt "frozen" or unable to move? That's because you awoke during REM sleep.

During REM sleep, your heart beats faster, your breathing speeds up, and your blood pressure rises. And yet you can't move. This is called sleep **paralysis**. That might sound bad, but during REM sleep it's actually a good thing! Otherwise your body would act out your dreams rather than rest.

Your Body Clock

Most of the time, your body goes back and forth very easily between sleeping and waking, and between NREM and REM sleep. That's because our bodies have a sort of clock that tells us when to sleep and when to wake. That clock is called our **circadian** rhythm (*circa* means "about," and *dian* means "day"). When our internal clock says it's time to sleep, our body processes slow down and we feel sleepy. When morning comes, our bodies sense that it will be time to wake up soon.

Electronic devices can disrupt your circadian rhythm, or sleep-wake cycle. They don't help you relax—they actually keep you awake.

Lots of things can go wrong with a person's circadian rhythm. One common problem is called "jet lag." When people fly long distances, they often have trouble resetting their sleep cycles to match wherever they are. Jet lag is an annoying but minor problem most of the time. However, there are many other sleeping problems that can be more serious. Next we will talk about sleep disorders—what they are, why they happen, and what you can do about them.

Text-Based Questions

1. What is the sleep cycle?
2. What are the main types of sleep?
3. What is happening to your body during REM sleep?

Research Project

Survey as many people as you can about how long they sleep each night. Try to ask people of many different ages. Then make a chart like the one below, showing all the different answers you received. What can you learn about sleep habits from these answers?

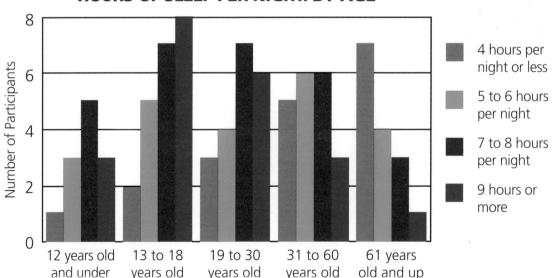

HOURS OF SLEEP PER NIGHT: BY AGE

Legend:
- 4 hours per night or less
- 5 to 6 hours per night
- 7 to 8 hours per night
- 9 hours or more

CHAPTER TWO

PROBLEMS FALLING ASLEEP

Words to Understand

acute: happening powerfully for a short period of time.

chronic: happening again and again over a long period of time.

dyssomnias: sleep disorders that relate to the quantity, quality, or time of sleep.

hypersomnia: being sleepier than normal.

Problems with falling asleep are sometimes called **dyssomnias**. The prefix *dys-* means "bad" or "difficult," and *somnia* means "sleep."

Just about everyone has some type of dyssomnia at one time or another. As long as it only happens occasionally, there is no reason to worry about it. But if sleep problems happen every night or continue for a long period of time, serious health problems can happen.

Sleeping Too Little

Insomnia can be caused by being upset about something going on in your life (this is called "situational" insomnia) or by some other physical or mental issue. Sometimes there is no obvious cause.

For someone to have a true insomnia disorder, she needs to have trouble falling or staying asleep at least three times a week for at least three months. People of all ages can have insomnia. It is a bit more common among females than males.

ARE YOU SLEEP DEPRIVED?

The National Sleep Foundation lists four signs of sleep deprivation in people under the age of 18. Do you often

- have trouble waking up in the morning?
- become irritable late in the day?
- fall asleep during quiet times of the day?
- need to sleep for long periods on the weekends?

If you have these symptoms frequently, you might be sleep deprived.

How insomnia is treated depends a lot on the specifics. Is the insomnia **acute** or **chronic**? Is the person healthy in all other ways, or does she have some other medical problem?

Sleeping Too Much

Sometimes people fall sleep a lot more often than they should. This is called **hypersomnia** (the prefix *hyper-* means "too much"). People with this disorder tend to fall asleep quickly and for a long time. They can be very difficult to wake up. They can also be grumpy or groggy for a long time after waking. And no matter how much they sleep, they still feel tired. It seems that no amount of sleep will be enough to make them feel energetic.

Lots of people dislike getting up early—especially teenagers! But if you have a *huge* problem waking up in the morning, you may have a sleep problem.

Problems with hypersomnia can be caused by a physical condition—including an injury or a brain disease. Being overweight can cause hypersomnia, as can alcohol or drug problems. Bad sleep habits can also cause hypersomnia or make it worse.

Problems with Sleeping and Waking

Another type of sleep disorder is circadian rhythm sleep-wake disorder. This long name just means disorders that involve the "body clock" mentioned in chapter one.

For most of us, our internal clocks tell us to sleep at night and be active during the day. This is our circadian rhythm. We all have a bad night of sleep sometimes, but the next night we usually sleep a little bit extra so that we can catch up. Our internal clocks help make sure that it all balances out.

But when a person's internal clock is broken, things aren't so simple. People are sometimes unable to fall asleep until much later than "normal." Or they wake up much earlier. And no matter how tired they might feel, the balance does not get restored. There is no catching up.

Jet lag is one type of circadian rhythm disorder. Usually, it clears up on its own and is not a serious problem. But what if you flew in airplanes for a living? Jet lag might be minor to most people, but for pilots, it can become a big problem.

People who do shift work (that is, working at night instead of during the day) are also at high risk for these circadian rhythm disorders.

DID YOU KNOW?

Stress is the number one reason people say they have trouble falling asleep.

Opposite: Air travel can disrupt your circadian rhythm. On long flights, it's a good idea to take a nap if you are able to.

CASE STUDY: CARRIE

Carrie, a high school junior, used to be an active, high-achieving student. She sang in the chorus and was co-captain of the field hockey team.

Over the last month and a half, Carrie hasn't been able to fall asleep until 3 or 4 a.m. Then she has to wake up at 6 a.m. for school. During the day, she's so tired she can hardly think. She's become grumpy and irritable, and her friends say she is "checking out." But no matter what she does, her body will just not shut down. Then she sleeps all weekend to make up for the lost time. Her grades and friendships are all starting to suffer.

What's wrong? Carrie has delayed sleep phase syndrome (DSPS). Her body clock is off. In a later chapter, we will talk about what people with DSPS can do to reset their clocks.

One type of circadian rhythm disorder is called delayed sleep phase syndrome (DSPS). A person with DSPS is unable to fall asleep until late at night and has trouble waking up at a "normal" hour. DSPS is very common in teens (see case study).

Narcolepsy

A person with narcolepsy can't control when or where he falls asleep. Instead, he has what are called "sleep attacks." People with narcolepsy can go from fully awake to REM sleep very quickly.

As discussed in chapter one, REM sleep is usually the last part of the sleep cycle. People go through four other sleep stages before reaching REM. But someone with narcolepsy can drop into REM sleep at any moment.

People with sleep disorders have to be extremely careful about getting behind the wheel.

A person with narcolepsy can have "sleep attacks" anywhere—while in class or out shopping, while playing sports or mowing the lawn. Think how dangerous this could be if it happened while you were swimming, or driving a car.

BREATHING PROBLEMS AND SLEEP

Some types of dyssomnia do not involve falling asleep. Instead, they have more to do with staying asleep and the quality of sleep people get. People with breathing-related problems can actually stop breathing while they sleep—sometimes for just a few seconds, but sometimes for a minute or more.

Breathing-related sleep disorders are quite common. According to the National Sleep Association, 12 million Americans stop breathing every night. Most wake up when they snore, which starts them breathing again. But they also wake up the next morning feeling very tired, with no memory of what happened.

If you—or someone in your family—snore frequently, it is a good idea get checked out by a doctor. There are treatments that can lessen the breathing problems and improve sleep.

If you don't get enough sleep at night, it can be very hard to pay attention in school.

This is especially scary because REM sleep is when we dream. Because people with narcolepsy skip the first part of the sleep cycle and go into REM, to them it can feel as though their dreams are completely real.

Text-Based Questions

1. What does dysomnia mean?
2. When does a mild insomnia become a disorder?
3. What is narcolepsy?
4. Name two circadian rhythm sleep-wake disorders.

Research Project

We know that teenagers need more sleep than younger kids. Studies have suggested that kids would be better off if elementary schools started earlier than they do and high schools started later. Find out more about this issue. What are the pros and cons of this idea?

CHAPTER THREE

PROBLEMS DURING SLEEP

Words to Understand

parasomnia: problematic actions, emotions, and thoughts that happen during sleep.

process: as a verb, to act on something in order to change it in some way.

somnambulism: sleepwalking.

The last chapter looked at problems relating to the mechanics of sleep, particularly falling asleep and waking up at the right times. Another group of sleep problems, **parasomnias**, relate to what we do while we are sleeping.

Nightmares and Terrors

Doctors believe that when we dream, our brains are probably working through emotions or problems experienced during

In 1799 the artist Francisco de Goya made an etching of the creatures that visited him in his nightmares. The text says, "El sueño de la razon produce monstruos," which means "the sleep of reason brings monsters."

CASE STUDY: KEVIN

At bedtime, Kevin just couldn't lie still. This awful, "creepy crawly" feeling in his legs wouldn't go away. His feet itched. Then both legs felt prickly.

He tried rubbing his feet together. He tried wiggling them. He tried kicking, stretching, and shaking his legs under the covers. Nothing helped. It was no use—he'd never get any sleep.

Kevin's symptoms are signs of restless legs syndrome (RLS). Doctors are not sure why some people get RLS, although it does seem to run in families. If you have symptoms like Kevin's, talk to your doctor: there are some medications that you can try, and sometimes basic changes to your habits might help. Regular exercise, yoga, baths, massages, and even warm and/or cold packs can also make a difference.

the day. That is, we **process** our daytime experiences during the REM phase of sleep.

Sometimes dreams are thrilling; many people dream of flying, for example. Sometimes dreams are uncomfortable; it's common to dream that you have to take a test you didn't study for. And, of course, sometimes dreams are frightening. We call these dreams *nightmares* or *night terrors*, and they are completely normal. Everybody has bad dreams sometimes.

Some people, however, have nightmares constantly, and their dreams make it difficult or impossible for them to sleep. People with this problem will sometimes avoid sleep because they don't want to have the nightmares. Doctors have defined two general types of disorders related to bad dreams: *nightmare disorder* and *sleep terror disorder.*

Nightmare Disorder. When someone has a nightmare disorder, she wakes up quickly from her terrible dream, and she tends to remember it well. The scary feelings caused by the dream—plus all that sleep that's lost by waking up so much—cause the person a lot of problems during the day.

The most common nightmare involves being chased. This nightmare could possibly be caused by the fear of a confrontation in your waking life.

Sleep Terror Disorder. This disorder is slightly different from nightmare disorder, because someone with sleep terrors finds it difficult to wake from the dream. When someone is having sleep terrors, he might toss and turn violently, sit up and scream, or even get out bed completely. He often can't be comforted by anyone else. And once he does finally wake up, he is usually unable to remember what made him so upset.

Like nightmares, having an occasional sleep terror—while certainly no fun—is not necessarily a problem. Still, it's always a good idea to discuss sleep problems with a trusted adult, such as your parents or doctor, just in case.

Sleep Behaviors

Sometimes people can be very active even though they are sound asleep. As mentioned before, these events are usually nothing to worry about if they only happen occasionally. But if they happen regularly, you should talk to your doctor.

Sleepwalking. This is the most common sleep behavior disorder. When sleepwalking, a person can get up and walk around the room, go downstairs, or even leave the house. Sleepwalkers can do simple activities, like eat, talk, or open and close doors. It is very difficult to wake a sleepwalker. Rather than try, it might be better to make sure that the person is in a safe space and can't use a sharp knife or fall down the stairs.

Sleepwalking (also called **somnambulism**) usually begins in young children between the ages of four and eight. Interestingly, among kids, it is more common for girls to sleepwalk, but among adults, it is more common for men to do it.

Dream Enacting. Chapter one covered how the REM stage of sleep, which is when we dream, involves sleep paralysis. This keeps us from getting up and acting out our dreams. But in some people, that paralysis gets turned off. People with this sleep behavior disorder will talk and move around as they dream.

It may seem strange, but some people are able to do simple tasks, like get food out of the fridge, while they are sleepwalking.

Dream enacting is rare, but it can cause physical injury to people who have it. Often it is more embarrassing to the person than dangerous. But, again, if a parent or sibling tells you that you've been acting out your dreams, it's worth discussing with your doctor, just to make sure you are safe and okay.

Text-Dependent Questions

1. What is a parasomnia?

2. Explain the difference between nightmare disorder and night terrors.

3. What are some things you can do to help ease restless leg syndrome?

4. If someone acts out a dream, what bodily function is not working properly?

Research Project

Keep a journal beside your bed and keep track of the following:

- when you fall asleep

- when you wake up

- how do you feel when you wake up

- what dreams you remember

- your mood and energy level throughout the day

After two weeks, review what you wrote down and see if you can find any patterns. For example, was a night of longer sleep followed by a more energetic day? Do you feel differently when you wake up and remember your dream, as opposed to days when you wake up and can't remember anything?

CHAPTER FOUR

TREATING SLEEP DISORDERS

Words to Understand

benzodiazepine: another type of medication, used to treat both sleep and anxiety disorders.

hormone: a substance in the body that causes an increase or decrease in a particular activity.

hygiene: actions taken to maintain good health.

hypnotic: the newest class of sleep aids, including Ambien.

psychiatric: having to do with mental illness.

When diagnosing sleeping problems, doctors usually consider four general causes: lifestyle choices, physical illness, **psychiatric** problems, and only after those are ruled out, genuine sleep disorders.

Lifestyle. Caffeine, chocolate, alcohol, and smoking can all interfere with the sleep cycle. So can having too much stress or too little exercise. One of the first things a doctor will ask is whether any of these lifestyle issues could be adding to your sleep problem.

Chocolate may be tasty, but it does contain caffeine. If you are having sleep problems, you might want to avoid it.

Illness. Some illnesses can interfere with the sleep cycle, including arthritis, bronchitis, and muscular dystrophy. Even something as simple as a broken bone can interfere with sleep, because of the pain it causes. If you have a medical condition that interferes with your sleep, let your doctor know.

Psychiatric Problems. It's easy to understand how feeling anxious or depressed can make it hard to sleep. But things like attention-deficit hyperactivity disorder (ADHD) and bipolar disorder—two conditions that are quite common among young people—can also affect the sleep cycle.

Sleep Disorder. The earlier chapters went over how sleep disorders can sometimes develop without any clear outside cause.

Making a Plan

The first step for someone with sleep problems is an honest talk with a health-care provider, who will ask questions about your habits and may run some medical tests.

Once a doctor figures out the problem, a plan will be made to address it. Some sleep disorders are so serious that people need to take medicine. For example, people with narcolepsy often take pills to keep sleep attacks under control. Doctors can also prescribe sleeping pills to help patients restore their sleep cycles. However, sleeping pills are a short-term solution: The goal is to help the body work better without medicine.

DID YOU KNOW?

According to the National Sleep Foundation, humans are the only animals that deliberately postpone sleep.

How Do Sleeping Pills Work?

Scientists have developed a number of different drugs to help people sleep. They each affect the brain in slightly different ways. But, in general, most sleeping pills work by quieting certain activities of the brain. In his book *The Promise of Sleep*, Dr. William C. Dement explains sleeping pills by comparing them to brakes on a car. Every brain, Dr. Dement writes, has a kind of "braking system" that can keep it from working too hard for too long.

Think about running a race. If you were running a marathon, you wouldn't run your fastest every single minute of the race. If you did, you'd quickly tire out and wouldn't be able to finish. To run long distances, you have to pace yourself. The brain is no different. Your "braking system" helps your brain slow down, rest, and conserve energy.

The chemicals in sleeping pills attach themselves to that brake system and force the brain to slow down. Drugs called **benzodiazepines** slow down the parts of the brain that control muscles and emotions. Newer drugs, **hypnotics**, are more specific, affecting smaller portions of the brain. This means hypnotics (such as Ambien) cause fewer side effects. They are also far less addictive than the older drugs.

Milder sleeping pills are sold in stores, or "over the counter" (OTC). Although these pills are easier to buy, they are still serious drugs. **Never take any sleeping pills of any kind without first having a discussion with your doctor.**

The Risks of Sleeping Pills

Both prescription and OTC sleep aids have downsides. Sleeping pills are strong drugs that affect the mind and body in ways that are not completely understood. This is why it's so important to talk to your doctor before taking any sleeping medication.

Overdoses and Interactions. Taking too many sleeping pills, or taking them along with other drugs, can make you sick or even kill you. Alcohol is very dangerous when combined with sleeping pills, because alcohol also slows down bodily processes. The combination of alcohol and sleeping pills can be deadly. Sleeping pills can also interact with other medicine you might be taking.

Side Effects. Sleep drugs can have unpleasant side effects. Some of the most common are:

- sleepiness during the day
- memory trouble
- dizziness
- upset stomach
- muscle weakness
- confusion

If you have unexpected symptoms after you take a sleeping drug, let your doctor or a trusted adult know right away.

More Sleep Trouble. Sleeping pills are designed to adjust your sleep patterns. But if you take the pills for too long,

I FEEL SICK: WHAT DO I DO?

Sleeping pills can be helpful, but they can also be dangerous. If you take sleeping pills—even if you take them when you shouldn't have—and you start to feel bad, there are a few things you should do right away.

- First, tell an adult. It's better to get in trouble for taking a sleeping pill than to get sick or die because you kept a secret.
- Call (or have an adult call) your doctor right away.
- If you are having trouble breathing, call 911.
- Report every detail of your reaction, no matter how small.
- Be honest: Tell the doctor if you took drugs or alcohol along with the medication.

they can change your sleep cycle. Also, when you have been taking the drug for a while, it will stop working as effectively. You will then have to take a higher dose, which just continues the cycle. The longer you take the medication, the more likely you are to have problems.

Hiding Other Issues. Sleep aids can improve sleep, but they can also mask other problems that may be causing the sleeplessness. For example, if you have depression or anxiety, your emotions might keep you awake. Pills might make you sleep, but they won't help you deal with the feelings. In fact, depression can be worsened by the pills.

SLEEP CLINICS

Doctors sometimes send their patients to special sleep clinics, where experts on sleep can run tests and help find solutions to various problems. If your doctor sends you to a sleep clinic, here is what you can expect:

- Your first appointment will probably last several hours.
- You will have a complete physical exam.
- You will also be interviewed by someone on the staff.
- You will probably complete a questionnaire that asks for information about your sleep habits.
- You might be asked to come back for an overnight appointment.

If you do need to go back, this is how it usually works:

- You change into pajamas.
- Wires are stuck to your head, chest, and legs. These will measure your body responses overnight, and they do not hurt.
- You may have a tube hooked up to your throat, to track your breathing.
- You will sleep alone in a darkened room, while staff monitors your sleep from a room nearby.
- In the morning, a specialist will look at your data and make suggestions about how you can improve your sleep.
- Then you go home!

Getting Better without Pills

Many sleep disorders can and should be addressed without pills. Doctors always examine other issues, such as personal habits, daily routines, and lifestyle choices, to find out if sleep can be improved without medication.

Sleep Habits. The first and most important thing to consider is what's called your sleep **hygiene**. In other words, the things you do related to sleep. Some things to consider:

Bedroom. Don't watch TV, text, or do homework while lying on your bed. Try and keep your bed for sleeping only.

Napping. Try not to nap during the day; sleeping during the day can hurt your sleep habits overall.

Sleep experts agree that good sleep habits should include keeping electronic devices out of the bedroom.

Chamomile, a flower that looks a bit like a daisy, is made into a tea that can help people sleep.

Food and drink. Sodas, coffee, and chocolate all have caffeine, which can keep you awake. Try to avoid eating close to bedtime. Alcohol can also have a negative effect on sleep habits.

Exercise. Regular exercise can help tire you out and also help relax you; both are helpful in improving sleep.

Supplements. Sometimes vitamins and minerals can be helpful for sleep problems. For example, people with restless leg syndrome sometimes take vitamin and mineral supplements such as iron, vitamin B12, and folate to help ease the symptoms. Herbal supplements like chamomile and passionflower are also used by some people with insomnia. However, these supplements are not regulated by the Food and Drug Administration the way medicines are. Always discuss taking supplements with a doctor first.

Melatonin. Did you know that your body has a chemical response to light and darkness? A **hormone** called melatonin is produced by the body when it's dark. Melatonin levels are highest in the middle of the night. Sleep researchers believe that melatonin plays a role in our circadian rhythm. Some people take melatonin to help regulate their sleep. The effect of melatonin supplements varies a lot: some people with insomnia think it makes a big difference, while others say it does not help at all.

Specific Therapies. Some sleep disorders can be treated using very specific types of therapies. One is bright light therapy, which is used to help adjust a person's circadian rhythm. This

Cherries contain melatonin, which helps regulate sleep.

involves sitting with a special light box that is about 20 times brighter than a regular lamp. Bright light therapy can also help with seasonal depression, which is when people get extremely sad during the dark, winter months.

Another specific treament is chronotherapy (*chrono* means "time"). Patients work with a sleep specialist to develop a plan that slowly changes the times they sleep and wake.

By combining these nondrug therapies with good sleep hygiene, many people may find that medicine is not needed

CAFFEINE

Caffeine is a drug that speeds up the body's processes. A little caffeine can make you feel more awake, but too much can give you headaches, make you agitated, and spoil your sleep. You probably know that there is a lot of caffeine in coffee, but you may not realize how much caffeine is in other things you eat or drink.

Food or Drink	Caffeine
Coffee (5 oz serving)	115 mg
Latte or cappuccino (8 oz)	89 mg
Jolt Cola (12 oz)	71 mg
Mountain Dew (12 oz)	55 mg
Iced tea (16-oz bottle)	48 mg
Regular or Diet Coke (12 oz)	46 mg
¼ cup semisweet chocolate chips	33 mg
Milk chocolate (1.5 oz)	10 mg
Chocolate brownie (1 oz)	6 mg
Decaffeinated coffee (5 oz)	5 mg
Chocolate syrup (1 oz)	4 mg

at all. For others, sleep-disorder drugs are an essential part of their treatment. In either case, most people with sleep disorders can be treated successfully.

Text-Dependent Questions

1. What are the types of sleep medications?
2. What are the risks of these medications?
3. What is good sleep hygiene?
4. What are some therapies for sleep disorders that don't involve medication?

Research Project

Choose one of the nondrug therapies for sleep medication, such as melatonin or bright light therapy. Find out more about it. What are the positives and negatives of the therapy? Why do you think it works or does not work?

Further Reading

BOOKS

Cuthbert, Timothy. *Be the Boss of Your Sleep.* Minneapolis, MN: Free Spirit Publishing, 2007.

Dement, William C. *The Promise of Sleep.* New York: Dell, 2000.

Foldvary-Schaefer, Nancy. *The Cleveland Clinic Guide to Sleep Disorders.* New York: Kaplan, 2009.

Schenk, Carlos H. *Sleep: A Groundbreaking Guide to the Mysteries, the Problems, and the Solutions.* New York: Penguin, 2007.

ONLINE

American Academy of Sleep Medicine. www.aasmnet.org.

Medline Plus. "Sleep Disorders."
http://www.nlm.nih.gov/medlineplus/sleepdisorders.html.

Narcolepsy Network. www.narcolepsynetwork.org.

National Sleep Foundation. www.sleepfoundation.org.

Series Glossary

acute: happening powerfully for a short period of time.

affect: as a noun, the way someone seems on the outside—including attitude, emotion, and voice (pronounced with the emphasis on the first syllable, "AFF-eckt").

atypical: different from what is usually expected.

bipolar: involving two, opposite ends.

chronic: happening again and again over a long period of time.

comorbidity: two or more illnesses appearing at the same time.

correlation: a relationship or connection.

delusion: a false belief with no connection to reality.

dementia: a mental disorder, featuring severe memory loss.

denial: refusal to admit that there is a problem.

depressant: a substance that slows down bodily functions.

depression: a feeling of hopelessness and lack of energy.

deprivation: a hurtful lack of something important.

diagnose: to identify a problem.

empathy: understanding someone else's situation and feelings.

epidemic: a widespread illness.

euphoria: a feeling of extreme, even overwhelming, happiness.

hallucination: something a person sees or hears that is not really there.

heredity: the passing of a trait from parents to children.

hormone: a substance in the body that helps it function properly.

hypnotic: a type of drug that causes sleep.

impulsivity: the tendency to act without thinking.

inattention: distraction; not paying attention.

insomnia: inability to fall asleep and/or stay asleep.

licensed: having an official document proving one is capable with a certain set of skills.

manic: a high level of excitement or energy.

misdiagnose: to incorrectly identify a problem.

moderation: limited in amount, not extreme.

noncompliance: refusing to follow rules or do as instructed.

onset: the beginning of something; pronounced like "on" and "set."

outpatient: medical care that happens while a patient continues to live at home.

overdiagnose: to determine more people have a certain illness than actually do.

pediatricians: doctors who treat children and young adults.

perception: awareness or understanding of reality.

practitioner: a person who actively participates in a particular field.

predisposition: to be more likely to do something, either due to your personality or biology.

psychiatric: having to do with mental illness.

psychiatrist: a medical doctor who specializes in mental disorders.

psychoactive: something that has an effect on the mind and behavior.

psychosis: a severe mental disorder where the person loses touch with reality.

psychosocial: the interaction between someone's thoughts and the outside world of relationships.

psychotherapy: treatment for mental disorders.

relapse: getting worse after a period of getting better.

spectrum: a range; in medicine, from less extreme to more extreme.

stereotype: a simplified idea about a type of person, not connected to actual individuals.

stimulant: a substance that speeds up bodily functions.

therapy: treatment of a problem; can be done with medicine or simply by talking with a therapist.

trigger: something that causes something else.

Index

Page numbers in *italics* refer to photographs.

About the Author

H. W. POOLE is a writer and editor of books for young people, such as the *Horrors of History* series (Charlesbridge). She is also responsible for many critically acclaimed reference books, including *Political Handbook of the World* (CQ Press) and the *Encyclopedia of Terrorism* (SAGE). She was coauthor and editor of the *History of the Internet* (ABC-CLIO), which won the 2000 American Library Association RUSA award.

About the Advisor

ANNE S. WALTERS is Clinical Associate Professor of Psychiatry and Human Behavior. She is the Clinical Director of the Children's Partial Hospital Program at Bradley Hospital, a program that provides partial hospital level of care for children ages 7–12 and their families. She also serves as Chief Psychologist for Bradley Hospital. She is actively involved in teaching activities within the Clinical Psychology Training Programs of the Alpert Medical School of Brown University and serves as Child Track Seminar Co-Coordinator. Dr. Walters completed her undergraduate work at Duke University, graduate school at Georgia State University, internship at UTexas Health Science Center, and postdoctoral fellowship at Brown University. Her interests lie in the area of program development, treatment of severe psychiatric disorders in children, and psychotic spectrum disorders.

Photo Credits